Where Do I Live?

Neil Chesanow

Illustrated by Ann Iosa

For Rachel and Rebecca Clifford

Library of Congress Catalog Card No. 95-8463

Library of Congress Cataloging-in-Publication Data

Chesanow, Neil.
 Where do I live? / by Neil Chesanow ; illustrated by Ann Iosa.
   p.   cm.
 ISBN 0-8120-6541-7 (hardcover). — ISBN 0-8120-9241-4 (pbk.)
 1. Geography—Juvenile literature. [1. Geography.] I. Iosa, Ann,
ill. II. Title.
 G133.C455   1995
 910—dc20   95–8463
                                                               CIP
                                                                AC

PRINTED IN CHINA

19 18 17 16

All inquiries should be addressed to:
Barron's Educational Series, Inc.
250 Wireless Boulevard, Hauppauge, NY 11788

International Standard Book No.
ISBN-13:   978-0-8120-9241-7
ISBN-10:   0-8120-9241-4

Date of Manufacture : March 2010
Printed in Shenzhen, Guangdong, China by Wing King Tong Paper Products Co. Ltd.

Where Do You Live?

You live in your _room._
There may be lots of rooms where you live.
But one room is special.
It has your bed in it, and your clothes, and your toys.
It's where you wake up each morning, and go to sleep
each night, and have sweet dreams.
When Mommy says, "Play in your room,"
you know which room she means.
That's what makes it special.
That's what makes it yours.

4

You live in your home.

Your home is the place where your room is.

It's the place where you live.

Of course, you don't live at home all by yourself.

Other people live there with you.

They are your *family*.

That's what your home is:

the place where you and your family live.

You live on a special piece of land.
Do you know what land is?
It's the stuff you walk on.
It's the ground.

For some people, this special piece of land
is called a *yard*.
If you live in a house, your yard is the land
around your house.
It's your own private place to play when you're outside.
Your yard is land that belongs to you and your family
and nobody else.

8

If you live in an apartment in the city, you may not have a yard.

The city has lots of buildings, so there isn't room for too many yards.

But the city has a special piece of land called the park.

The park is a nice green place to play when you're outside.

A park is *like* a yard for people who live in the city.

A park doesn't belong to only one family.

It belongs to everyone.

You live on your street.

Your street is black or gray and it has cars.

It runs right past the home where you live.

Your street runs past many other homes as well.

All the homes are next to each other.

The street belongs to everyone who lives next to it.

Everyone who lives next to a street can say,

"This is my street."

You live in your *neighborhood*.
Your street isn't the only street there is.
There are many streets where you live.
All the streets are lined with homes, just like yours.
All the streets and all the homes that are near your
home form your neighborhood.
That's what a neighborhood is:
a group of streets and homes where people live.

You live in your _town_.
Your neighborhood isn't the only one there is.
There are lots of neighborhoods where you live.
All the neighborhoods that are
near each other form a town.
That's what a town is:
a group of neighborhoods in the same place.

Your town has the market where you buy food.
It has the bank where you get money.
It has the school where you go to learn.
It has the post office and the library and
many other things besides.

All the people in all the neighborhoods _share_ what the
town has, just as you share toys with your friends.

You live in the *city*, the *suburbs*, or the *country*.
Where is your town?
There are three places it may be.
One place is in the city.
The city *is* a town: a great big town, or a group of
towns that got so big they grew
together and became one.

Another place your town may be is in a suburb.
A suburb is land that's around the city.
The city has more people.
A suburb has more room.

Or your town may be in the country.
A suburb is land that's near the city.
The country is land that's farther away.
The country has the fewest people and
the most room of all.
Enough room for farms and
forests that take up lots of space.

You live in your state.
Your town isn't the only one there is.
There are lots of towns where you live.
All the towns that are near each other, and
all the land around them, form a state.

A state is a really big piece of land.
Dotting the land are dozens
or even hundreds of towns just like yours.
Every town is made up of neighborhoods, and every
neighborhood has streets and homes where you and
all the other people in your state live.

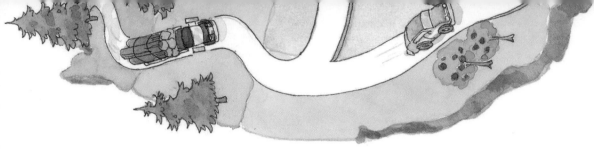

You live in your country.

Do you know how many states there are?

Fifty!

That's a lot of states.

Together they form your country.

That's what your country is: a group of fifty states.

All the states treat each other like very good friends.

They do things together, just as you and your friends do.

Together they build highways, share water, keep the land from getting dirty and spoiled, and many other important things.

That makes them something very special.

It makes them *united.*

They're united because they do things together *as one.*

Being united is what makes the fifty states one big country.

Guess what the name of your country is…

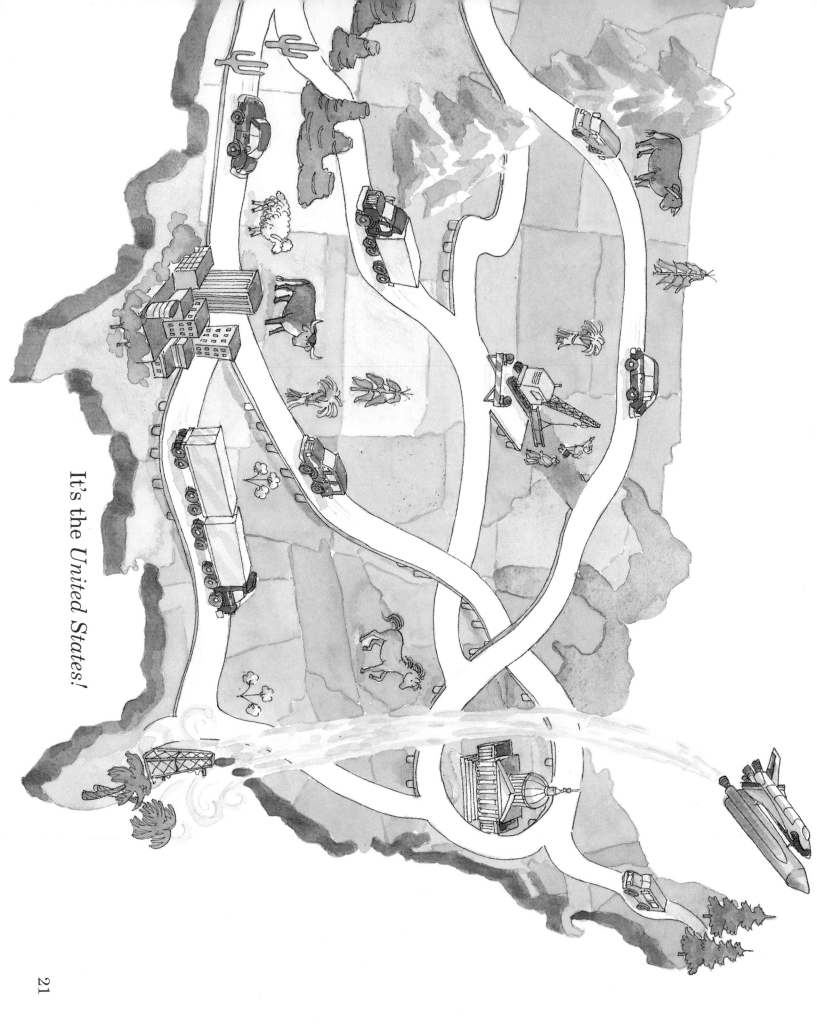

It's the United States!

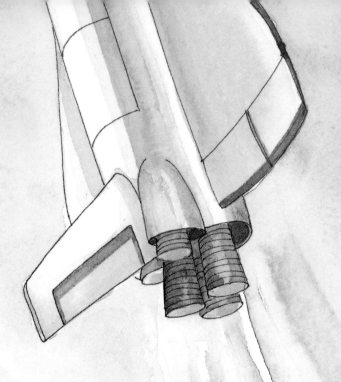

You live on your continent.

A continent is a huge huge piece of land.

It's much bigger than a state.

It's usually much bigger than a country.

A continent is so big you'd have to ride a rocket ship way up into outer space to see one in person.

The continent you live on is called North America.

North America is so big it has three very large countries on it.

You can see what they look like in the picture on these two pages.

This picture, and many others in this book, have a special name.

They are called *maps*.

A map is a picture of land or water or even the sky that shows you where everything is.

The map you see here is a picture of your continent.

It shows you where all the countries are in North America, and what they look like.

At the top of the map is the coldest country.

It's called Canada. It's up north.

At the bottom of the map is the warmest country.

Its name is Mexico. It's down south.

Your country, the United States, is in the middle.

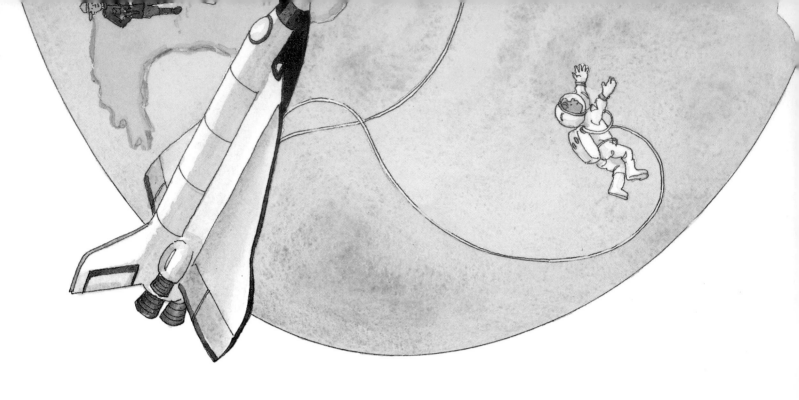

You live in the *world*.
North America isn't the only continent there is.
There are seven continents in all.
They are all huge, huge pieces of land.
Most of the continents are like North America.
They are divided up into countries where people live.

One continent isn't like the others.
It doesn't have any countries.
It's much too cold for people to live there.
Instead of being covered with countries,
it's covered with ice and snow.

Do you see all that blue around each of the continents?
If you think it's water, you're right.
The water around the continents has
two special names.
The bigger bodies of water are called *oceans*.
The smaller bodies of water are called *seas*.
Just as there are many continents,
there are many oceans and seas.

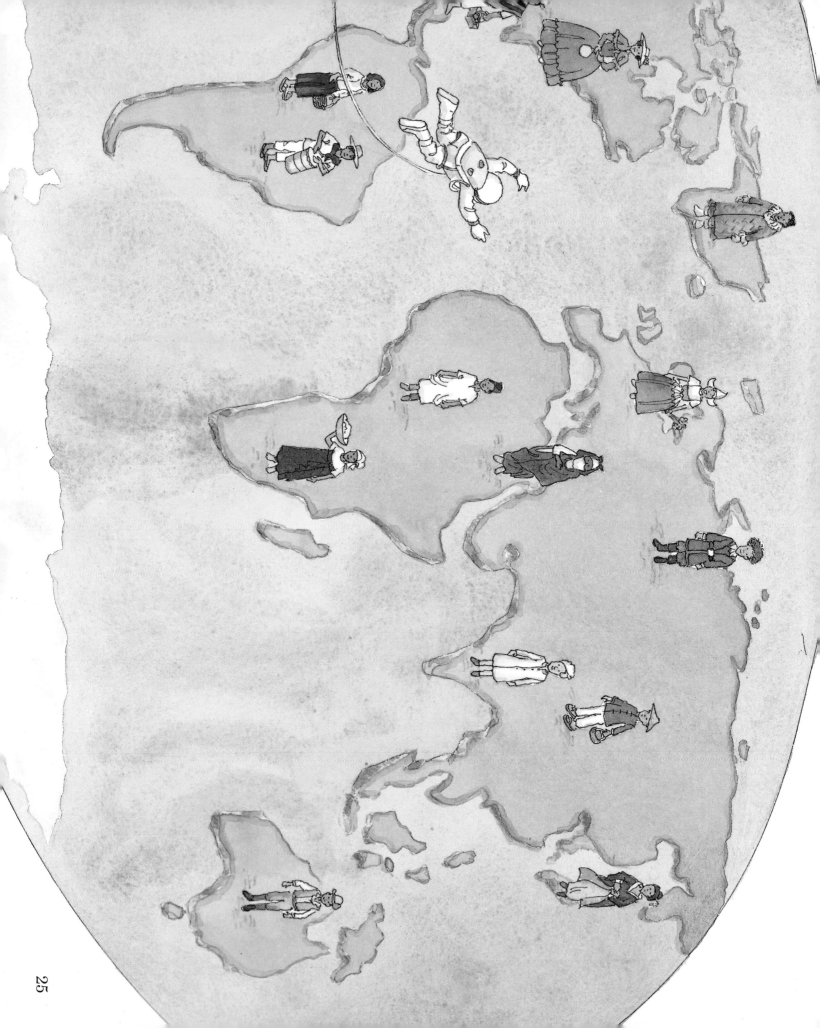

You live on *Earth*.

The many continents are huge, huge pieces of land.
The many oceans and seas are even bigger bodies of water.
That's what your world is made of: land and water.
Your world has a very beautiful name.
It's called Earth.

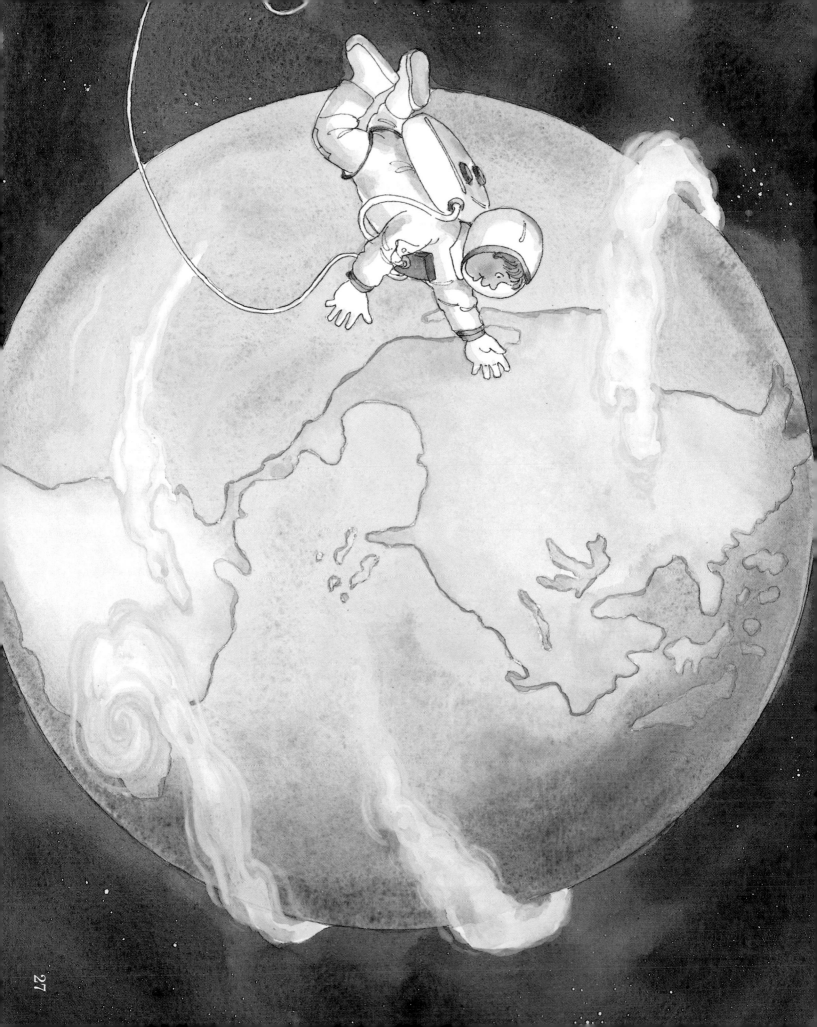

You live on your *planet.*
Earth isn't the only world there is.
There are many different worlds.
Earth is a special kind of world called a planet.

A planet is a big fat ball in outer space.
This big fat ball does only one thing.
It spins around and around in a great big circle.
It spins in a great big circle around a special star.
The name of Earth's special star is the *sun.*

You live in the *solar system*.

Earth isn't the only planet there is.

There are nine planets in all.

Nine big fat balls in outer space.

They all spin around the sun in great big circles.

Together, they form the solar system.

Solar is just another word for *sun*.

A *system* is a way of doing things.

One way to do things is to spin around

and around in great big circles.

It isn't a very good system for people—you'd

get dizzy—but for a planet, it's perfect.

That's what the solar system is: Earth and the

other planets spinning around and around the sun.

You live in a galaxy.
A galaxy is a gigantic group of stars.
Millions and millions of them.
Way too many to count.
You're going to love the name of the
galaxy you live in.
It's called the *Milky Way!*

The Milky Way not only has millions
and millions of stars, it also has Earth's
special star, the sun, and the nine planets
of the solar system.
The Milky Way is so gigantic it seems to go on forever.
But it doesn't.
Big as your galaxy is, it still isn't
the biggest place where you live.

You live in the *universe*.
The Milky Way isn't the only galaxy there is.
There are billions of galaxies.
They all have way too many stars to count.
Each galaxy is so gigantic it seems to go on forever.
But it doesn't.
At least, not all by itself.

Together, the billions and billions of galaxies
    make up the universe.
The universe is the biggest place there is.
If you can't imagine how big the
    universe is, don't worry.
Nobody can.
That's how big the universe is:
much too big for anyone to imagine.
It's the one place that really does go on forever.
And you live there, too!

You live in lots of different places—*all at the same time.*
And they keep getting bigger and bigger and bigger.
You began in your cozy little bedroom.
And you ended up at home in the
biggest place of all: the universe.
The universe is so very, very big that it holds every
other place where you live.

Can you remember all the other places you call home?

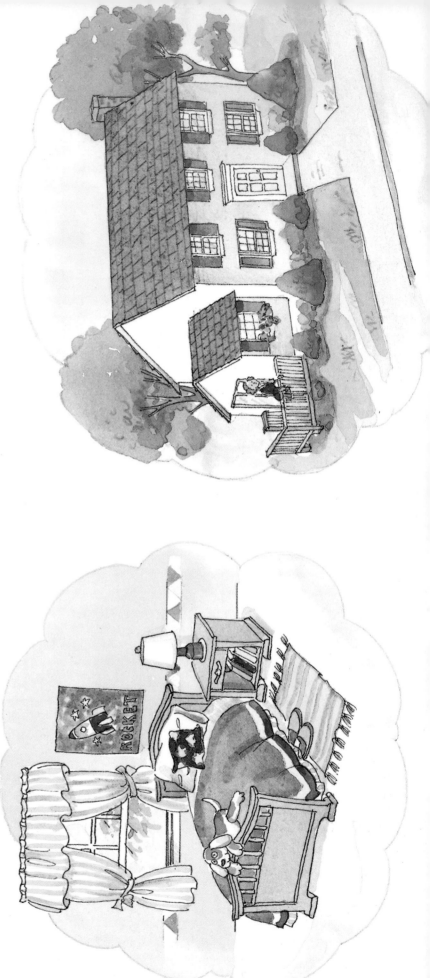

The galaxies full of stars.
Including your galaxy, the Milky Way.

And the solar system with the nine planets
spinning around and around the sun.
Including your planet, Earth.

And the world of Earth, with its
seven continents and its many oceans and seas.
Including your continent, North America.

And all the countries on all the continents. Including your country, the United States.

And all the states that are in your country.
There are fifty.
Ask someone which state is yours.

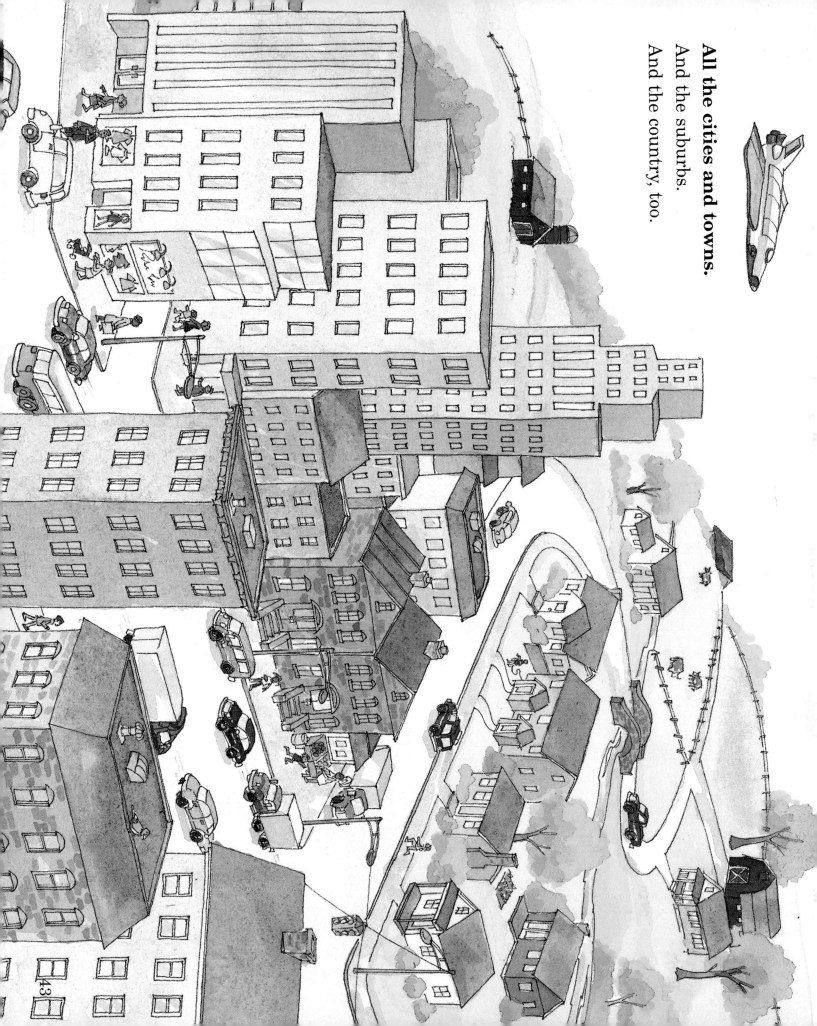

All the cities and towns.
And the suburbs.
And the country, too.

43

All the neighborhoods.
Uptown, downtown, north, south, east, and west.

44

And every home on every street there is.

45

Including yours.

And that's where you live!

47

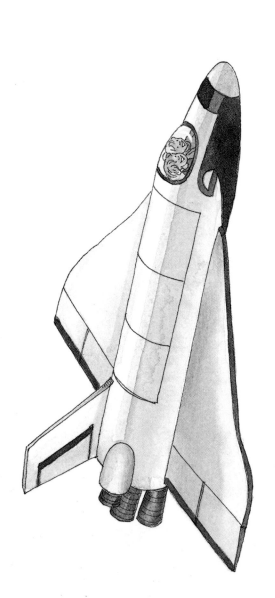

How much do you know about where you live?

This is the number outside my home _____

This is the name of my street _____

This is the name of my city or town _____

This is the name of my state _____

This is the name of my country _____

This is the name of my continent _____

This is the name of my planet _____

This is the name of my galaxy _____

This is the name of all the galaxies together _____